Dedication

I dedicate this to the young man named Chance because everyone needs to have a chance to learn who the Lord is. This is the one thing Chance would want you to know. Don't take a chance without this also all power belongs to the Lord. He has the gift of everlasting life to share.

This young man may have only lived 25 years but he gave an impression of a lifetime of living to me, and others who loved him, within those short years that he lived.

The truth is often hidden like a shadow in darkness but there comes a time for disclosure.

How many people do you owe that will tell you, "You owe me nothing now. We can settle up our debt in the next life."

We see into mankind's life; one person at a time. But only God can truly see into their hearts.

Thank you
Bro. Bush,

Along with his partner and friend, Chance Tate

Welcome to All

The introduction to what could be the only way the USA may be able to save face in the presence of the whole world.

Now let's get busy and save the jokes for later in the year 2017, because that is how we are being looked at like we are a joke.

This is why we have received this message; to give us a chance to change; believe it to receive it.

How Can This be?

This occurs by a process of growth that people in the USA did not stumble upon that has more than two levels within it. It can help improve one's self, along with the best way to bring the country back to a kind of glory that we the people can truly be proud of ourselves from using what we had within us that became one of the greatest things knowing we help in the most important ways as the Lord wishes. That way we bless the Lord on the throne and country gets blessed back.

We are in line to repair the potential problems at the RNC to stop the darkness and madness; also the personal one of not taking a stand as the governor over the hired service people in government, that we the people put in place to do the job we hired them to do that we are responsible for, like it or not.

We the people are the ruling class of people that have been appointed by the Lord to be the overseers of the government and it got turned around because of shiftlessness and the people's abandonment of their post that mankind was appointed to be in charge of.

That is what we must make a comeback to if we want the country to come back. It is our obligation if we don't the country cannot. We will keep stumbling around without a true vision of a right minded purpose.

Now it will be up to you to divide and conquer the individual way to help yourself to have control over the life you have been entrusted with.

Once again Satan got sucker punched with a one-two and got knocked out of something before the beginning of the RNC. He even saw it coming but he couldn't get out of the way because the Lord is the opposite. He comes straight to you and Satan almost always blindsides you.

How did it happen? It is long story made short– the people needed to become their own heroes and the Lord presented them with a plan to get a halos. They got them by having faith in themselves that they could freeze a part of hell over and that will take one of the biggest steps that has been taken by a multitude of people in over 2,000 years, or around this amount of time.

What gives them power over darkness? It could be said that they gave themselves a chance first to start the process of freezing a part of hell over that wants to show up and show out and bring out the foolishness in as many people as it can?

Next, they learned that we are coming into a brand new level wisdom to do what adults in the body of Christ are required, as was meant to be that, we have been passing the buck about and complaining. Then to make it all bad, American people are auctioning off the USA as well as acting like the Israelites and wanting a person what think they are some kind of king and cannot see what they are wishing for and are not being careful about because of what happened. The USA can get the same kind or ruler as Israel got, when they begged the Lord for a king, only with a different twist that could bring trouble to our country's doorstep.

Now if we take one problem at a time and get the first one right we will not have to work so hard because it gives insight to put the county on a winning state of growth by doing what may be different like us starting the wiping of our feet at a time when we felt threatened by a process gone bad or a threat of a riot. As I said, people that are feeling this negative kind of thought would wipe their feet on the ground and say "Satan this is your knockout blow to keep you down and out and the hell you want to raise at the RNC or in the Cleveland area is dead to the upper world and that hell has been frozen over to keep it in the lower place where it won't harm anything or anyone, in the name of the Lord."

If you would like to know more about how your support can help get the complete information, buy a copy of *A Promise to Help Prevent Violence at Protests and Rallies in America!*, at Amazon.com (in eBook format) or at Createspace.com eStore (in printed format) or to help with promotions to get the good news out and with other kingdom building, there is a GoFundMe account available, www.gofundme.com/nzp42cys, to receive donations.

Hello, if you had a pound of prevention that would create a miracle, what would you do with it? Is this the preventive measure from the Lord that prayers have brought forth? Do not try to figure it out. Come see or just get it to know it for yourself.

May Peace be With You!

The arrows are flying that are shot out by the army of the Lord's cupids. What do they say? Hello to you with love. What is there mission? To help anyone in need with special categories with the last seven books, titled *A Promise to Help Prevent Violence at Protests and Rallies in America*, *The Ending Political Wars in America*, *The Devil Passed Me By*, *Ending Spiritual Warfare in America*, *Fixing What is Broken in America*, *The Disconnection of Extremism*, and *The Recovery of the U.S. Government*. This one makes eight that have been recently authored by Bro. Tracy E. Bush. To find others visit www.boundtoheaven.org.

At Bound to Heaven Publishing/Ministries, we are keeping it better than real. There is no way any of us can really afford this wisdom. We are truly blessed with a gift from the Lord and this is the bare bone facts about it.

As a confession of my shortcomings, it is still humbling for me to write without ever receiving a formal education. Now that I have been accepted by myself what can I do to make my service stand out? What can I do to influence people to get the information? What will motivate the all people in the right way that develops the contagious courage to want to learn something off of the beaten pathway?

For anyone who knows there is a shadow of the devil on or around you know this; there are others who know it also that are good people. Don't try to figure it out just get rid of it.

Right Up Front

To help keep you in tune with learning, let's say whatever you think you know you may not know about sometimes. Now that your mind is open, let's get started.

If the Lord has a kind of insurance policy for us it would be foolish not to try it!

Who Am I?
I am an exalter of the body of Christ Jesus; for his sake

The writing I do is to exalt the Lord so you will know of his love by way of what he does. Protection that may come by way of pleading the blood over the love you have for Jesus that he has for you.

Do you know who God is? You may know his act but do you know his thoughts as Moses did. If not, become a student by way of the Holy Spirit. He lives in you and do you know that part of you?

Life is no condemnation, joy, peace with love in the front and love in the back of us.

This may be one of the first social experiments on a spiritual level to give people a new way of learning how to stop or head off a problem.

The thing I am not so sure of is when it works could it be not just from a sense of reward by way of a blessing but by means of a self-psychological presence of transformation that we preserve through our own positive visions that mankind makes come true. That goes the same way that is being done or called into existence that makes problems and troubles.

Now if it works what will happen in some people that are carnal, it was done by man not by God because they have been trained or brainwashed by the wiles of Satan in the ways as a people are trained to think. That is all that it takes to get us off track.

Then mankind's big problem is they don't want to accept the truth because they don't want to be made wrong. My thing is let's get it done and if you are a believer when the devil passes us by, then you make up your mind.

We are the kings and if we get the devil cast out of us, then the pastor has the means to counsel us and the politicians are the servers of us. Then if the Lord tells us what to do ask God what it is and do it because he will tell you.

Now if we don't do what we are supposed to do, what do we expect? Could be anything! Therefore kings and queens it is time to know your job is to become the rulers of the country.

We as people are in danger of rerouting ourselves back to a king as if we were a people living under the old style English Kingship process. This has been turning the people in America around to the way we don't want to live. Therefore, as a people we can and should wake up and walk out on ourselves in the placement of the way we have been letting ourselves live in a darkness of a kind of ruling that is heading for an ungodly kingship that is leading man and we the people who are to be led by the Lord fail ourselves and the country.

Now, if we don't vote for the right person as commander in chief will become a king and take our jobs and break down the system that hurts people.

The Lord Will Let You Know

The Lord will let you know that you are supplied with the shield of wisdom to make it impossible for your enemies to penetrate the covering of love that the Lord has an endless supply of. The use of it comes to protect people who love the Lord because he loves them and that gives power to defeat the enemy.

One of the greatest lessons we can ever learn is if we know there is a part we play in the battle the Lord shows us how to do what we are to do in a way that keeps us safe. He never meant for us to totally sit on the sideline and watch the fight.

He wants us to see what he does through our imagination and do what we do through our imagination also. That is why we have it because it can take us there in the battle with our mind and heart in order to see our way to defeat the enemy and win the challenges that we are confronted with in our lives.

Therefore, lift up your shield over your head to protect you and others from the flaming arrows that will be fired upon you in the crowd of people to protect all who have come to voice their opinion. The fire will be put out because the shield has a water power on it to drown the flame. The presence of coolness will prevail. There will be light where Satan wants darkness the show will go on without the drama that the blind people who follow Satan wants to happen.

We can't let ourselves be defeated. The number one reason we have to set an example for the children that depend on us. The Lord has left them in our care and we can't let them be led astray from the Lord by Satan. This has happened enough. We have lost too many of the younger generation and it must stop.

We have disappointed the Lord long enough as a people. It is time we stop using so many excuses to not do a thing but sit on our asses and complain. Then wait and watch and sometimes front or perpetrate to be seen and will not get the work done because we have not studied to make ourselves approved. If we don't do that how in the world can we fix or become one of the Lord's repairmen/women. Someone is always breaking something.

Well, get in a course of study. If you won't pick up the Bible, get in some kind of wisdom teaching plan. I have developed one that has different levels. The beginner plan gives you the insight to crawl on all four limbs before you start on two. After you complete that you will have your wings and halo.

The good part is you can get started today, to become a disciple to the Lord's will in your life.

For more information, etc. order the books you need to work with today. Thank you with the blessings of the Lord.

What man meant for bad, God means for Good!

The leader can be the imagination helper to explain what to do to get it done the right way.

I can't tell you better than you can learn it for yourself. The way out of the traps that Satan sets for all people in different ways have one thing in common, they are meant to harm them, steal from them or a part of them. They feel they can't get back to lie to them, create fear in them or kill them.

Well, the time has come to let he who is greater than you cast out all unwanted demons out of your life. You have the tools, you know how to use them and there ain't no time like the present, to get the gift of freedom!

The books I suggested can be ordered online at boundtoheaven.org. What can these books do for you other than take your mind off of self and put it in touch with the diamond jewel in yourself to polish the outlook on the future you wish for all people? The wish is for you to know of a new freedom to join into a fellowship and feel equal to the people you live with and worship with. The wish is to show the way to someone who may not be able to see the truth to know how the use of wisdom works to make things right in the dead of the night without his salvation.

So you can use the power of good over evil. Rational thoughts, irrational thoughts and fears and worries come to you and get them out of your head...get rid of them!

Thoughts that are elevated so high it controls people. They get controlled by towerism.

Breaking Thoughts Out of Captivity

Thoughts that don't come from the word can hold you in captivity. Therefore, we pull down strongholds. Put off or take off a strip out of the old thoughts and put on the new man.

Who are you in the body of Christ? When will you fix your mind to transform who you are not to what you think you should be; a human that has heavenly value that may replace the old you with a new you.

Will we give up any or the rest of God conscious that calls us to use or lose our kingship, to a dictatorship. Now if we are not learning. Therefore, does the candidate causes the fire to begin to burn in the way of confusing people that can harm them. Then they want the fear to jump in place in people and at the same time they want to act like they are putting it out.

Do they act like a bad boomerang that harms people and come to the forefront to become the fire chief to put out what they started up in the first place. Now, if it looks like a phony and take like one them it's one. Therefore may your eyes be open to the truth. Because in the time of crisis people turn to Christ.

Now, if we don't know we can learn that the trade-off of a demonic person that looks good has presented this time and time again to ourselves. And if we are not carefree we fall prey to ourselves and that can't be blamed on anyone.

This game is as old as Rome itself. Therefore, if you are still a lamb of God, you won't mind shearing the wolf's wool off of you. Therefore, it might help you to get a copy of a book, _A Crown for Kings and Queens_, and get a copy of the _New Wise Men_ and _A Calling to Become Watchmen for God_.

Ephesians 4:20-24
20. But you have not so learned Christ,
21. if indeed you have heard Him and have been taught by Him, as the truth is in Jesus:
22. that you put off, concerning your former conduct, the old man which grows corrupt according to the deceitful lusts,
23. and be renewed in the spirit of your mind,
24. and that you put on the new man which was created according to God, in true righteousness and holiness.

Philippians 4:8
8. Finally, brethren, whatever things are true, whatever things are noble, whatever things are just, whatever things are pure, whatever things are lovely, whatever things are of good report, if there is any virtue and if there is anything praiseworthy-meditate on these things.

Psalms 91:1-2
1. He who dwells in the secret place of the Most High shall abide under the shadow of the Almighty.
2. I will say of the Lord, "He is my refuge and my fortress; My God, in Him I will trust."

Now what can all this mean? There is nothing missing or nothing broken in life that cannot be repaired!

To the Kings and Queens

There is a place that is secret to all but you. It is a room that is within you called a secret place. It has a throne in it and it is there to worship whatever you put in that seat. People don't know it and the only thing that belongs in it is the Lord, not you as some people think belong there themselves as those with towerism or the rich people that wealth becomes too much for them. It gives them no control of self.

Now, if you put the problems of life in the throne seat it is what you are worshipping do you understand? Protect the throne with the wisdom of the word of the Lord. Don't get caught sitting on it. Don't place anything on it just worship it and pray that the Spirit of the Lord that is a part of all people finds favor to sit in it within your secret place to pronounce the blessings upon your life, that all mankind wishes, hopes and prays for day and night.

The one thing about it you must know. You have to guard this secret place on the inside of you because it is like the upper room. This is a must do and it is your responsibility. It is like having the essence of the presence of a peace of heaven in one's self.

The way it works is when the job is done right by you, the Holy Spirit looks out for you in return and when the Lord looks out for you, there is no greater being in all the lands to have in your corner.

Why is it that Americans have been losing ground? It has not protected the throne room of Christ in one's self. The people are unwise and letting Satan weigh into the place of sanctuary. It is so many defrauding the part of America. This opens it up to attacks by domestic and foreign people and the only way to save ourselves from this kind of indictment of a spiritual war is to fight back by uniting with self then with each other.

People have to stop being two faced about their life and acting like it is okay or alright and it is not. If you don't know the Lord you don't know yourself no matter how you twist it up or down IN your life. People need to understand if you are being two faced to yourself, no one will ever know, mother, father, sister, brother, or a child of yours. The only one who knows this is the Lord and if you don't know yourself, you may not know crazy as it song its truth; Oh Yeah, Satan knows.

This is a part of the blinding at birth method Satan has been applying to people's lives ever since he did what he did in the Garden of Eden. But now that it is known he can no longer blind us as a people on this level, we have a chance to win greater wars that are in our way. We can continue to increase the process in the body of Christ. Amen and Hallelujah!

Can we really afford to not take a chance to learn to apply truth to our life? If we may have a better chance to succeed to make life better this may be the only chance we need to have to become as one in the body of Christ where we have failed at and are failing at.

Therefore, let it be known, do not let the chance pass us by. Apply it to your life, it may be just what the doctor needed to show you the way to a better life on earth and turn the present state of disarray in the country and people around. Furthermore, it will help you to know who chance is and how he helps you now since we get so many chances. There is only one that matters; that is the hookup with the Lord.

That one chance to go to meet and greet and see what chance has done for you and others because he is waiting for you at the gates of Heaven…believe and receive that. Don't take a chance on missing out of being with chance.

God bless you and all of yours!

In recognition of what a mighty chance he has given to us.

I Pledge

Satan, for the pain you cost me, my family and friends I turn it back to you. No more pain; I have fixed my brain and heart in Jesus. I have learned not to learn any more from the prince of darkness. I have let the Holy Spirit turn my life inside out and outside in, to clean and clear it of the unseen filth and dirt, in order for me to let a change come into my life to see the mighty working of the Lord in me in ways that I never gave a chance to be a part of my life, as it is and needs to be. Again, I thank the Lord for a chance to make myself whole and complete.

This is a part of God's promise that is in lots of places that it should have been taught, it didn't. It is not to think about why not. It is to spread the left out process of the gospel that we rejoice to have in our present day to delight in to bask in the old way that the Lord has seen fit to share with us for the edification of the love he has for us. We can never be as worthy as we need to be to become a part of his kingdom in Heaven. But because of who he is and how much we mean to him, the love he has for us surpasses our understanding.

That is why we give thanks to the Lord daily in that secret place he has in us and in fellowship and praise. If you don't know, now you know. What Satan meant for bad, the Lord meant for good.

This is a pathway to grow when you see wrong, do right. When you think wrong, give yourself a chance in life to think right. This is all it is about. We make mistakes and that is a part of being human. Change and stop that process of living because there is only one way in and one way out. Don't make things where you don't have a chance to get out the right way. The beginning.

Extra, Extra, Read All About It!
Satan Got Kicked back to Hell and Back Again!

Now only if you don't or didn't know how to defeat the part of Satan that comes to harm you from the blindside you know now. Stand up with the Lord and you can see him coming and then watch the Lord at work.

What's Going On, Again?

Stopping the ungodliness of Satan, one person at a time, by revealing his play book on how he can cause chaos and confusion in the USA using the political arena as a boxing ring for the country to get into a fight with each other. But first the demons of darkness have to show people how to lose the inner fight by not accepting the truth. Then a part of a war has been won.

It is now a time of crisis that we can head off to defeat. We can do this by not allowing ourselves to be tricked or fooled in a way that may, first of all, hurt our pride. That is right, if it is a time in life to stop and dump your pride the time is or may be now. I can't say any more about that because if we want to continue to live in a free democracy, we have to take a stand against ourselves personally.

The north and south winds are going to collide again. I mean that the quickening of a pawn used by Satan that has the sound of a duck that doesn't know how or when to be careful of what they say is inciting violence. They do this to bluff people into letting them have their way. This is someone who doesn't care if all hell breaks loose and is not an adult. They are a kid (as in goat) that has no sense of being a peacemaker like a child of God would be.

They are groups of people who are not capable of maintaining a stable atmosphere. They want to create fear and think they are in control. The sickness of towerism is like being a tower with a certain level of actions they have because of the out of control power and strength they want to create that only exists in their mind and not in the real world for the sake or real benefit to mankind.

To get back to the danger of this, the last time on a major scale such as this that gave me the ungodly feeling of a war of a kind that is of an in house; one as I will use the USA as the house. When the north and south had it out; at the end of it was the most disproportionate death tolls of ugliness. Even worse, the dead soul sin-drome that captivated the nation was so bad the number of lost souls that couldn't find their way to heave was very large.

The people in the south had to employ a man of God to help with freeing the wickedness of some of the spiritual loss in death of the stench of death that could not move on to the light to lead them to their reward.

If Satan has a toehold on you in any way and victory comes to the wrong person that comes into office as the president. If you are lost already you may think you are a winner and trap yourself even more into a time that give you light but end with death.

This is a kind of spiritual war. It is not a joking matter. It could permanently scar some people and leave them hell-bound. The rising up of some of the same old dead spirits are ready to become attached to whomever they can and take the ride with them to wherever they go along the road to death.

Now is the time to do your homework. I have written about this before in earlier writings, as part of the 40 plus books I have written to date. I have worked with the Holy Spirit to help show a better way of life.

Again, first get in right with self. Then get out of the spiritual war that can be ending soon. One person at a time wins this war. Please be one of those people.

Ask not if you don't want to know
the fear of the Lord in actions within you.

Now if you didn't know before, you do know now who to ask. But remember to not ever want to be a part of the Lord letting his permissive will fall upon your life.

Take Notice

The Lord is still seeding the messengers with his word that said let his people go but not to the Pharisee and others but straight to Satan who may be residing in people who are somewhat unknowing of this.

Know now that you don't have to fear this. You are not alone if you take the extra presence of what his developed within you that may have been placed upon you as a curse of the forefathers or mothers who didn't know how to stop this from happening.

It is time to rejoice because the day of liberation is yours to have and move you forward in a great way without being stuck to get to a promised land. First it is to know of the land within that is made out of earth, then the land without of you that you have already arrived upon.

Don't get choked up off of this you can swallow it!

This is a way to teach people how to put on their own brass knuckles because there are two different wars that they are in to win.

Thank God no one needs to be a wolf spider. It must have been a pet created for the devil only.

Now After the Dust Settles
Let's Get Some Other Kind of Work Done

Pick one or take this one. Stop the act that can give us as a people in this country more work done by the elected officials in Washington, because they should not be fund raisers on the time clock when we are paying them.

That may be one reason we are lagging behind in getting things done. The time wasted may one day be time needed. To take it one step further is this some kind of crime that steals from people because they make the rules? Then we should help by making inside laws before they pass. The people need to know so we can do something about them if they are not of a just cause. Or could it be they do let us know and we don't check on the things they do anyway.

If so, then it is up to us to know if we want it or not. That means to stop passing the buck and the shiftlessness has to stop and as we are called to do jury duty we should be called to do Bill passing and checking the credibility of job performance on an on-call basis to go with it. That will be a good start to put a plan like this in order.

Therefore, who will step to the plate and start the team development process because when you have a team it doesn't make it so hard and it can be like the right kind of dream come true.

There is a shortage of one thing we hope and pray you help us fulfill and that is common sense because we need more of this to go around. Can you help?

There is a non-authorized suggestion of a book written by someone else. It may help the thinking of all people. A book authored by William J. Federer titled, *America's God and Country*. If you have a chance, read it.

Never let your crazy thinking overrule your sanity.

Zero in Not Out - Don't Duke Yourself

Muse News

Big thinking to do but I will.

The One Thing

I hope no one thinks my writing is too raw.

Words

If you walk the walk you don't have to talk the talk!

It is so nice to see someone so full of love you may think they don't know what they do with it; yet God does.

The Lord said he would never leave you or forsake you but you can forsake him and leave him.

Love =   Limited or Longsuffering
                    Off or On
                    Victim or Victorious
                    Ended or Endless

You can help by offering up your prayers. Thank you for any or all the help you can give. Sincerely Bro. Bush

Adventure Road

This is an annex to What's Going On? If you are in need of an anecdote to an undetected sickness to come, I may have one.

What in the world am I talking about? First, if there is not a contested issue about the candidate D.T. in Cleveland, Ohio due to the people who voted for him at first look at the pre-arranged plans to stop a war on a spiritual level that can hit people on earth.

What is to Come is an Un-tie Your Mind Process

If we look at it as they gave in, does that mean that the people got so enraged with the political system as if they would rather let it go to hell or through hell before they stay on the same old pathway they may put anyone in office.

Now that is one dimension to this equation. The next is the politicians' bluff got called out by the needed spirit of change has got to come or else we might as well start all over from having a kind of disaster. This was number two.

Now does it stop a problem that may have caused a fight in the country by him D.T. winning? Yes, but if that is the case of non-contested nominee D.T. Did the Lord allow the foolish to carry on to the point that it wouldn't be a spiritual war going down.

So now what happens due to the presence of the people change their position to give another party a chance to run the country for the next four years? So do we show the world that the country that should have made a female a Commander in Chief before everyone else, in the world but there was no on taker. Also because of how things was supposed to be set up in the first place as a free democracy so all can do it or not depending whether they are qualified.

I say this because we bull-crap all over the Bill of Rights that was put in place, the equal rights amendment was down played and forfeited on time and time again. It took a living hell to come to life before the people in the tower had to stop slavery as an example.

Now do we need a revelation of an unearthly kind to see our way clear out of this new kind of darkness or are we sensible enough to walk into the light that has been given to us as you may not see but some do, noting the RNC may take 100 years to rebuild itself behind a D.T. attack if it goes all the way. Before the fall the pride has to be kicked out or else.

Therefore, can we take a break to put on breaks for a minute and even if it is necessary to become a no show at the time of the convention.

In other words, leave one's self out of the process, and forget the costs because it is not that serious to have a loss like that, that is known to say you are fired anyway. Now what does that mean you won't get a damn thing done anyway, even the blind can see that but if you think you can out think the wiles of Satan that has latched on to some people you may be in for the ride of your life. The politicians are best at their kind of personal warfare.

Therefore, if you are heading for the greatest location in the nation, know there is love waiting here. But you have to understand that your heart has to be transformed to the righteousness of mankind and not of self-kind.

As an author, I do have reservations about the large number of towers people coming to the City of Cleveland, Ohio. The last time I was coming from Ocean City, Maryland, at the time of 911, my trip got detoured because of the plane that tried to hit the Pentagon. I will say, not being pretentious, I felt insecure.

Now to take it to a place where I have been in my writing before, which I live: home is where the heart is and if home is Cleveland, Ohio, then I look at it as my adopted motherland, even though I was born in the backwoods of Mississippi.

The point I am making is not my fear but the premonition of warning of a state of darkness that needs to be handled. The explanation of this is at a time long ago I had a dream that the same people who killed my friend's mother was going to kill my mother. In the dream I was shown who it was and I helped put a stop them and to this problem.

Now before this incident it was another killer who got away and they never found out who did it. The killing was done on a strip of land that was called Kingsbury Run. Now at the time I was shown who was doing the ungodliness, it happened in the somewhat same script. But it was never brought to light because the killers were caught and I helped. Besides, it was in an area around a bridge I was fond of.

In saying this, another killing just occurred this week, April 25, 2016. Now what else can I say about this? One of the main killers was named Hightower, back in the time I helped, between the late 60's or early 70's, because of this. I feel it is my job to help people down out of towers instead of letting them fall down on someone else, as they have been doing in the USA since the country began.

Now how much farther can I take this presence of thought as far as I let myself because it is truly endless. I think when I get to Heaven the Lord will have a desk and chair, pen and paper, waiting for me to do what I do.

My point is we can still keep developing love but as I say learn how to lose and don't get sore about it because everyone gets in the win column at one time or another in life and losing may be winning.

Here is information about the only waterfalls in Cleveland

To present this as carefully as
I know we have seen a runaway train!

When traveling to the waterfalls, my friends and I often went by way of riding a train, hobo style. As a boy, I used to ride the trains to get to the waterfalls and back home. When we missed the train coming back it was a long walk.

Now if we are riding the train which way are we going, east to west or west to east? Now it doesn't matter because we are either going to the waterfalls or coming back. That is right, the only waterfall in the City of Cleveland was a retreat and a long trek back in the day for a group of kids that lived in the bricks b.k.a. Garden Valley. The waterfall was and still is the only waterfall inside of the City of Cleveland. As a child it was beautiful. As an adult, it is even more beautiful.

If you don't mind, I would like to share a little more of my lifetime. I learned at an early age, the power of high in life. It somewhat made me feel like I was the king of the world. It did not help me at the time when I took a trip at an early age up in the terminal tower. The train left from Union Terminal in downtown Cleveland and ran to Meridian, Mississippi. It was the Union Railroad passenger system that no longer runs from the Terminal Tower. While on several ski trips to Durango, Colorado, I had the privilege of riding the Silverton Train around and through the mountains.

At the age of 4-5, I first crossed the bridge. I began leaving home at age 3 and a half, at least two to three times per week to make new friends. My mother and father mostly had to look for me or call the police. Getting back to the bridge that is formally known as the Sidaway Bridge that looks over a part of land that was made into a valley in time where the greenest grass had ever grown. That gave a presence of love. Now if you need to know a presence of love you know what to do to get it; no bones about it. It was okay but the best high I got from going up to a high place was going across a bridge. That is right, I lived about ten minutes walking distance from a bridge.

Of course, I was told by my father not to go on it or across it. But, as a child who was used to adventure and between the city and the country life, I had a fascination for it. One day I went to it as I had done time and time again. I saw a guy that had come back from across it and they had lots of potato chips, pretzels, etc.

I found out at the other end of the bridge there was a place called Dan-Dee. Now at the time I asked where did you get all of those goodies from they said Dan-Dee. I made up my mind I was going to see who this was and after a period of time, it was less than one month, I made my move.

I crossed the bridge and when I did I saw a white man (who could have been Polish) and I said "Do you know Dan-Dee? I came across the bridge to get some potato chips." He said "this is Dan-Dee, the place you are looking for. But the chips cost money." I said I didn't have any money. He said "If you listen to me and do what I say, I will give you some bags of chips." I said okay and he told me when there is a green rag hanging on the fence by a truck I can come and get the bag with the chips, etc. in them. But if I don't see a rag or him, don't come. I said okay.

This happened for about two months. I would go on a Friday or Saturday morning. One day I took a friend with me and he didn't listen and went to the trucks and took a box of chips out and someone saw him and we had to run for our lives.

At the time the bridge had gotten old and had gotten old and had some missing boards on it. If someone had fallen through, they would probably die. That ended the free chips. I never went back again.

If anyone would like to know where the bridge is, all of us that went across it knew it as the swinging bridge, it's proper name was the Sidaway Bridge. Here is the description and location. It is Cleveland's only suspension-style bridge. It is a pedestrian foot bridge built in 1931, spanning a ravine known as Kinsbury Run, connecting Sidaway Avenue to Kinsman Road, near East 72nd Street. The bridge was 680 feet long, 105 feet high and 6 feet wide. It connected Slavic Village and Garden Valley Estates. In 1966 a feud between a Polish-American group on one end and an African American group on the other caused someone set fire to a wooden deck and planks from the southern end of the bridge were removed. It is a graceful looking structure that can be restored.

At that time, I lived off of 75th Street and Kinsman Avenue in Cleveland, then moved up into Garden Valley at the top of the hill. That is why I had access to it.

This is the place that helps me feel good about crossing as a child by myself. Now there is a demon possessed person out in the somewhat same neighborhood as I was partially raised in. This brings me full circle to want to stop all the madness in the world I can. Can anybody help? Maybe someone can have a dream as I had and identify the killer.

The next bridge I had a thing for was the Old Kinsman Bridge that had special arches on each side. My friends and I had a thing for walking up the arches and they were about 60 feet high. The wind would blow and we would have to lay down so we would not be blown off, which would have killed us. The bridge was torn down and rebuilt, without the arches.

Finally, there is was a bridge that is now the bridge from Broadway Avenue to Broadway Avenue, Turney and Warner Roads. As a child that bridge looked very different. We would look up to it from the Waterfalls.

Intermission is Over

Here is information about the bridge of faith that still stands:

Bridge of Faith

Break time is over. I must find my way back to the point but I had to take a look out of my back door first to see the falls and glory it still has.

Now if I seem like I am all over the place with my writing, I am and to know why I will try to explain. First it is to try to build a bridge for people to cross and not have fear of falling off. If a wind blows too hard, the bridge can swing and we want to not create danger. Second, we want people to see the vision they need at the top of the bridge to look out over the beauty it can show you if you let it. Finally we want people to make the right decisions.

Let's say if the ill wind has blown people off track in their thinking and the not so grand has shown up to smell like a dump, what can be done about it? Well everything and that is the good part of life.

We always have a chance to stop the madness that leads to sadness and sometimes all we need is faith. Let's take the hand that has been dealt to us in the voting process: to know how much we need change we have become delusional as humans.

Tribute

Therefore, "let's go crazy" on the dance floor only and "let's get nuts," and wait for what has been put up to come that could be a great hit." We may have lost the creator of those hits but only in a physical way. As it is known; we keep each other alive through our memories, to help keep us enjoying the hits after they are gone and it doesn't get any better than the impression that his spirit left by the sight of a rainbow.

Get this: to slow walk the process and get the bull to the market it got bloody and I have been in the presence when my grandfather and uncles had to load one on a wagon in the south, it had a ring through its nostrils that bled like hell. I decided it was too much for a kid. Therefore, I kept my distance from the bull because I didn't like the actions they are able to perform.

Now to take this to the real world, if I feel the b.s. of someone it left me to believe it is the same way. It contained pain. Therefore can I do anything to stop the pain that people have? Well, I helped stop the murderers who raped and killed my friend's mother so my mother would be safe.

Now I use my pen sword to stop as many demons of the spiritual world that I can. The train can't be derailed in the process of America. The way things are turning out may be good because what mankind meant for bad the Lord meant for good.

M-N

The people in the United States should stop acting like the government is their parent because in the Lord's eyes we are supposed to be the parents of the government. It is time to stop going up and down the hills and valleys backwards and turn around to see the level ground that is right before you.

The facts have been worked out beforehand if the D.T. gets what he wants in the first process of being the GOP nominee. This is only what could be a way to end the unnecessary government b.s. that the people don't want, also to help with the process of there not being a violent protest and rally in Cleveland, Ohio.

We have won a war that people have helped to win in an unorthodox way I must say I am impressed. How will the rest of the political arena come to order will they not support their candidate? Or will their voters not elect the RNC's choice as president? Or Will we see a new level of fear and darkness come into power that raises up an ungodly stench the world can turn their nose up at to not like the people for putting an incompetent chief at the table for them to have a deal with?

It is not a kind of czar that people need to lead them. It has been tried before and it doesn't work. Now it is up to the people to know it and to stop the downfall of a place that is not to be looked at as a third world country.

That is right, some of us act like that is where we want to be and that is what a derailed mindset is. But to go to the bright side we can let people make mistakes and talk about it to improve the system we have in this country.

Don't bring the towerist to the table because they will be in charge of what the people will have to eat. Additionally, the English part of them will come out in the wrong way. I don't' want to think how ugly that may become.

It is my dream to see this land I love kept in an even more pristine way for all of the future generations to know and see the sights I have seen, from the woods of Alabama and Mississippi all the way up to the Rocky Mountains and through Canada. In retrospect, if you don't know by now that we can stay winners in America it is time you do.

What could be my goal for this to see if there is one who has a greater ability to dream a dream that outweighed the ones I have, to give them insight that grows a spiritual reflection of the inner blessings that show a way to love. Additionally, for all people to prosper and to know what it is and when it is revealed - what could be what the truth is along with a process to a culprit of ungodliness to help with the process of stopping them.

The Lord can reveal a person who is living by demon-logic principals they live by, if they don't want help. Now if there is anyone who doesn't fear this kind of blessing, step up to the plate; the Father, Son and Holy Spirit is waiting for you. Now this can be the right time to identify yourself to find out who you really are that can allow you to move on.

A Message to the Brethren
I Did But I Don't

There is a troubling fact that hurts me: why people in the house of the Lord sometimes act like they are so high and mighty? They even act like if you don't come to them panting for and desiring the privilege of being in their presence, as a person in total need of them. They act like you don't exist or more so you get treated with no respect. It is there "click" thing that they almost require you to crawl up to and somewhat make them think you think highly of them.

The wrong they do to people gives me a sick gut feeling because they forget who they are servants to as the Lord requires of them. They have put themselves upon the pedestal of a level of towerism that they can't see the love for a man and a state of common touch and want to fool people. It may be the pathway they are given to know the will of God in their life has developed a flow that they refuse to see.

I have felt a distancing by the clergy in ways that only the Lord has carried me through, even in some of the largest churches in Cleveland, Ohio and some on the outside of Cleveland. They know who they are and please don't treat others as you have treated me. The Lord will remember you being ugly.

The Ecumenical House of God and Church Without Walls,
(to share the traces of pain helps it go away)
Bro. Tracy Bush, Founder and Shepherd

To My Family

I do apologize if I do offend anyone but I have the right to express myself and the way I feel I have to let out my grief after the loss of a loved one. I don't mean to become so personal in the state of such a serious life matter issue that included the growth of our country. But I will make this as short as I can.

The death of a person is a personal process of outgrowing the grief of missing them. It hits people in different ways. I have found that it hits me in ways that go from one end of the spectrum to another in growth also. The process of my father's death was brief and painful. The process of my mother's death was, no grief, some pain but a lot of growth. Why was it so different? I believe it was because of the actions that followed and the desire that was left for me to do as they might have wished for me to do.

My father wished for me to take care of my mother, brothers and sisters and that was about all. My mother kept establishing kingdom building, placed a news house of God one earth to let the Lord shine his light on people so they would know the Lord and how much he loved them – enough for them to confess their sins and accept him as their Lord and Savior.

This I did in a community that a man of color had never done before. Now it is a place that I can say the people who give love to you will also keep giving it and if you don't think you are getting it, it may only be because of you needing more of what it takes to let the message come in and that is only one thing the spirit of the Lord.

The spirit of the Lord can grow in you to a level of the will of the loved one who his gone can help you do what the Lord wants you to do and what they may have wanted to do also. In saying all of this, it is my belief that a man named Chance wanted the country to give a chance to the women of the world to let them be all they can be.

In stating this I say I do like the sometimes to quacking duck but he has too much iodine in him to will the kind of will that the American people need to have in their presence and if the country gives him a chance to do a job if you have never prayed, you better start.

Even though this book and its contents is somewhat dedicated to an anti-violent process, it is an ongoing growth of a process that may start in one place but it keeps going year after year in order to increase people's chances for a better life.

The Growth and Development of Me and Cleveland

We have to look out for the future that needs us to keep it moving in the right directions for the protection of people and what we have built. I have been an activist and have helped to clean up a part of negative things in the old style street revolution with some of the real soldiers of peace. That helped started the movement, such as Bro. Omar Ali-Bey and Bro. Harlell Jones. There are more that are not named. I have been involved in the past with protesting and in training programs with Bro. Khalil Samaal and more. I have been endorsed by a number of clergy members and have worked with them in their community-based efforts to improve the lives of others. I have participated in projects and programs addressing family matters with Pastor Walter Humphrey and others. I have been given acknowledgment from the City of Cleveland and other local organizations for the work I have done in the community.

I been endorsed through words of encouragement to keep the faith that the Lord is going to find his way to use what I am doing for the edification of the body of Christ by Dr. Otis Moss. I have spoken at the SCLC, the Men's Day Program at Fellowship Baptist Church, St. Paul AME Church and at the Baptist Ministers Conference. I have done television and radio programs in the past, for example with Stanley Tolliver radio program and on television with Harry Boomer of channel 19/43. There were others but none of this do I hold dearly to myself than to hear the sounds to come that say I have done good in the work I have been called to do by the Lord.

If you think anything is missing, it isn't. The rest of it may be found in one or more of my writings. On a personal note, my name, Tracy has the following meanings: American – "warrior," English – "fighter," French – "harvester," Irish – "bravery," Old French – "courageous."

Who will claim their spiritual domain?
I hope it will be all of mankind!

The name of this bridge that cannot be seen but can be crossed is life everlasting. You want to make sure that you take the necessary steps to get across without fearing anything but not crossing it.

Now could all of this be a part of the new parallel universe to come?

Is this something that has the same presence like the crossing at the red sea if the people did not cross or stopped in the middle of it they would parish!

The Lord has made a crossing.

Don't fear crossing this bridge. It has been built with and up from love!

People now have an opportunity in America to correct themselves and the country. With the help of this information, people can be a part of helping to open the flood gates of Heaven so manna can rain down! At the least or best it is a blessing!

Could we look at that as if a new frontier has to be discovered that mankind has not wanted to get too deep into in order to save face? I guess no one wants to be embarrassed alone. Therefore, if people act like something doesn't exist, things are okay even if they are not. that is why we are doing something about it: sharing spiritual skills. You can find more information regarding spiritual skills in an upcoming book titled, *All Peoples Handbook*.

This all adds up to the elements we seek to free us from the petrified forest that is a gateway that Satan stands guard over to enter hell.

At the free stamp in downtown Cleveland as a part of the winning team with the B-ball game. I talk about the winner in the books before it came to pass.

The people are not complaining about the fact the city being known as a city with a curse. Now how will they feel about the new blessing.